ARRIVING
IN MAGIC

Also by the author

'The Call of the Unwritten' Poems 2010

'The Mark Widdowson Blogs' Prose 2013

ARRIVING IN MAGIC

Poems by

ADRIAN G R SCOTT

authorHOUSE®

AuthorHouse™ UK Ltd.
1663 Liberty Drive
Bloomington, IN 47403 USA
www.authorhouse.co.uk
Phone: 0800.197.4150

Published by AuthorHouse 10/18/2013

ISBN: 978-1-4918-8159-0 (sc)
ISBN: 978-1-4918-8168-2 (hc)
ISBN: 978-1-4918-8160-6 (e)

Now, arriving in magic, flying,

and finally, insane for the light,

you are the butterfly and you are gone.

And so long as you haven't experienced this: to die and so to grow,

you are only a troubled guest on the dark earth.

The Holy Longing by Johann Wolfgang von Goethe

For my children

Eva Katharine	27th April 1991
Lara Francis Hope	23rd October 1992
Thomas Donald Gabriel	17th November 1995

Contents

Arriving in Magic

Why do I always turn to the stone
to try again for a king's sword
when wizards wait out in the wood
set to make of me a master?
Again and again I am snatched
by flattery to step up and lead,
be on the team, sit on the board,
ignore the space that incubates.

No more can I pass the gap that gates
the path unnoticed, stepping through
towards mossy trees and fish's glimmer,
novice to the green flame in the bud.
This magic is the fierce embrace
of all that makes up our life's course,
uttered bold in faith to the deep
unsleeping witness of the dark.

That unyielding and steady gaze lays
bare the me I really am and
not the me I would have you see.

Finding the dragon's shadow dancing
vast on my small room's wall and see
how often I've pinned its tail on you,
and as his scales form bright on my skin
I inhale richly his secret fire.

An old skin sheds no longer needed,
a way of good belonging now
outdated, letting go its grip I
find my orbit round a greater force.
No more am I a hub for hubris
to build its castle on, no longer
a beggar for attention but an
owl-eyed hunter for the untamed space.

The ring you place upon my finger
is a vow to grasp the magic
in which gladly I now arrive.
Knowing too it was always there
waiting quietly in the trees beyond
with the wizard that is the forest
and inside, the dragon who is me,
the magician I have come to be.

I
Gateways

When will you be ready?

When will you be ready
to hear the voice
that has been speaking to you
with a patient kindness
for some time now,
like birdsong as you wake?

Don't mistake its kindness
for weakness, or insignificance,
it is neither, moreover the voice
is your most ardent, though from
a place you have not often
had the courage to visit.

Trajectories are strange, they
have an inertia, a momentum,
that makes you think they
must be right, they are the way,
yet often they are just a
form of sleepwalking.

I was once told of an alpine
photographer who, in order
to get the clearest views on
his Hasselblad camera would
switch off the engine and glide,
thus minimising the blur.

Only when you cut the motor
will vision find you, only when you are
ready to attend will your soul's map
unfold, only then will the path
you took make sense and the
way ahead appear out of the mist.

My Face

I often wonder what my face
says as it stares out at the world.
Is it begging a question of the
returning gazes, asking who am I
and where does my face fit?

Is it requiring permission to speak,
waiting for a teacher to open the
floor to my tentative lips as they
try to shape themselves around the
timid lines forming behind my eyes?

What are the secret signals my soul
is sending out? Can I overhear with
these cusp like appendages framing
my face, the message given out
and returned to me with interest?

Haste

You want to rush, get to the end
work it out and have it solved.
Who wouldn't? But the cost,
who pays the price of all this haste?

A friend of mine knew Mirabehn
Gandhi's English companion.
Her story; when the Mahatma
found himself without a pencil
she tore off to find it, returning
breathless with the prize and
was rewarded with the words:
'Mirabehn all haste is violence'.

Carl Jung was fond of this adage,
'all haste is of the devil',
he would sit and pause after
every sentence of his writing.

Those gaps, informed his genius,

as he mapped our psychic topography,

escaping the diabolical lie that

time is always running away.

Even the Roman Emperor, Augustus,

deploring rashness, for a logo had

a crab and a butterfly with the motto;

Festina Lente—make haste slowly.

Later the Tuscan Medici's Tortoise

with a sail on its back reminded them

of those vineyards slowly maturing

followed by a measured harvest

yielding their waiting's ripeness.

How much pain could we

save ourselves by recalling

every journey ends in rest:

death's sacramental comma,

why hurry towards it when there is

such bounty in the lives of those we rush past?

So much truth for us in the eyes of those

we try and fix with unseemly haste.

So much ripeness unharvested

when we gather in to soon.

So much to be gained when

we make haste slowly.

Lara's Surgery

The prospect of your surgery incised mindfulness,
drained the vein of present attention,
its callous date blacked into our calendar,
a fixed and fixing point in life's soft fluidity.

The courage I coached myself in
ebbed away at the memory of your birth,
sending you ten weeks before your time
into those life-supported, aching days of anguish.

When the parting veil of death wrapped
its viscosity round your tiny frame,
then released you back into this tender world,
where you gradually became indomitable.

Your face left stretched by your growing,
until your adult choice for surgery offered
another threshold where death grazes life
and we arrived that perilous space again.

A year of national health, pulling, breaking jaws,
pain, endurance, hospital wards, visiting times.
One operation negotiated, then onto the next,
top jaw forward 17mm, bottom back to match.

Yet by some grace or choice I did not take
this journey with the hooded gaze of my past
but with a wide-eyed owl-stare, a pledge
to go hunting life's spark in the present.

Until I finally found in your reshaped face
the unmet woman of my grown-up daughter,
the sweet smile so like my mother's and your
astounding ability to reinvent your future.

Initiation

The hug you gave me in that first moment
of diagnosis was vice like, sob racked.

Type one diabetes, at sixteen
a hammer blow and a terrible fear
realised in the time it takes
to go in and out of the surgery door.

Now you prick your fingers everyday,
that sharp droplet touched to the blue strip,
a trill pronouncing the amount
of sugar sweetening your blood.

Then the second wound, insulin in,
to the flesh of your stomach,
a place I once made raspberries
with my lips to make you laugh.

Initiation the ancient art
of wounding the boy,
teaching him that his bleeding could

become a place of wisdom,

that he needed to learn to weep out loud,

to wield his new found strength

in the service of something larger,

that he was part of a greater story.

What kind of a Dad do you need now?

One who has done his own bleeding,

who is not frightened by his own shadow,

who can call time on his own ego.

A man ready to start the next chapter called your story,

an on-going narrative that he will leave before it ends.

But Son, in the time we have left

can we embrace again like on that day.

Connected as men, sharing our pain,

at sea on a strange ocean,

initiated by all this unasked for suffering.

Distinct—your journey not mine,

yet for a time in the same boat.

Carried by the true tide of courage to a shore

I want to reach first and wait for you to join me.

Step One—I Am Mad

I am mad
to stand outside
on cold mornings
and smoke crafty cigarettes.

Then to take
vitamins and little pearls
of garlic and cod-liver oil.

To run
on a machine, or tramp
though the valley with my dogs.

I take
blood pressure tablets,
feel the squeezing armband
of my systolic over diastolic,
and always the tension of my madness.

This

is the frontline

between my presence

or my disappearance from this world.

I wonder

what would it be like to relax

and not hold the tension between the two?

Between

mother and father,

harmful or healthy,

pressure and release.

To hold

left and right,

dark and light,

to wait for the reconciling third—

the

one who

walks between,

offering

inner dilation,

deep appreciation,

radical acceptance.

Where life

breathes over me

in moments of tranquility

without the need for nicotine.

Could this

be the road of returning sanity?

The way

to pass through the aperture

of freedom to an unforced future.

Where I

no longer store all that anxiety

in my neglected body and then have to medicate it.

Where I

can breathe it all out in a moment of relief.

Where the

deepest breath will fill the lungs of my deepest me.

The Edge of Bleakness

There is an edge of bleakness—
a sinking in the pit of the gut,
that makes the future feel unsteady,
on your shoulder a perching unease.

The pressing question being what to do
with that edge, how to engage in
one of those deliberate journeys that
overfly the territory of uncertainty?

Then suddenly you know you need
to land, to settle into the hermitage
of unsolvedness, to wake and
pray into the offices of liminality.

Sometimes soon, often later, perhaps on
a moon-shadowed walk, or when eating
a meal of mindful bread you observe
an appearance, the return of a stranger.

Retaking its seat in the vacant space

it left when you ejected it, eyeing you

with suspicion, not quite trusting your

welcome, awaiting your first question.

If you can quiz this darkness of yours

with a tender curiosity, unpicking the

carapace of denial, receiving courteously

the gift that it is being returned to you.

Then you will have sweetened sourness,

undammed the gut's pit, emerged from over

the threshold of bleakness, arm around another

exiled shadow bearing more of your lost gold.

Ladybower

Ladybower dam sits in a great
Y shaped bed, reflecting her
bridges and hills, still and dark,
watering the people of Derbyshire.

She is like our selves—
at the confluence of many flows,
reflecting and holding great forces,
spreading skies and darkening depths.

For our lifetime we sit in our bodies
a disclosure of enclosed consciousness,
a village submerged under us and
flights of Dambusters passing over us.

To find a homecoming in our life
we need to go down to the times
that created a sharding, the drowning
of many memories in the lost town.

Or rise up in courage to face the
searing anniversaries of loss that
punctuate like air raids the most
ordinary of sojourns on this earth.

If we don't engage in these trials
then when the water recedes
the drowned ghosts will emerge
from the doors we thought closed.

The bouncing bombs will fall, breaching
those carefully constructed personas
that passed for identity, leaving us stranded,
arid and unready, bewildered by our plight.

Mercifully it need not be the end
in fact it could be the beginning we need,
the dam can be reconstructed by our
willingness to sit in the empty space.

To trust that a potency greater than
our own will pour in around the depth
we discover in the ruins of hubris, then
we will be a reservoir for the thirsty.

2
Path Crossings

I Am Me And You Are You

That young girl of your school uniform carried,
like an apprentice Atlas, the ubiquitous anxiety
which your parents handed down to you.
That girl had no quiet, no books to feed on,
no stories in the famine blighted house just
a picture of a Mother cow chewing all the grass.
Your spinster Aunt's house a bolt-hole but
no real antidote for the fears you fell heir to.

And now that lost girl of your anxiety sits
in the corner staring at the young boy of mine.

I broke my teenage arm on a bike no handed,
asking a young boy am I okay?
'I think you broke your arm', he said
I fainted, stood up and fainted again.

Unsteadied by a Father's departure I couldn't trust
life not to take my Mother too, I was not okay.

It seems we are the marriage of inherited dread,
the convergence of unchecked anxiety,
overcoming us both, the only cure a generation back.

Up the attic stairs through shafts of dusty light
to my Grandma's room drinking tea, strong and old,
playing a child's game; 'I am me and you are you'
she would intone and in my glee I answered;
'No I am me and you are you', an endless litany
of silly self-assertion knitting us together.

A Norfolk farm girl, she came to London
to be a kitchen maid, she married the boy
who came to wash the dog and carried through
the blitzed and shrapneled streets two daughters
to end up in the attic of my boyhood house.

Up your road, with the aunt's, in a white house,
your grandmother, a whale boned Lewis woman.
Carrying her life in her face, three grown children
in her strong arm's grip, the Husband too quickly
torn away caught a pearl in those island eyes
as she read her solitary scripture by a nightly light.

We bear the memory of those two fearless women
an antidote to the congenital anxiety of our parents.

In the choosing place which is now our marriage
will we shrink back into anxious shadows or walk
forward towards a pain filled, joy chorused life,
where I am me and you are you and that's enough?

Visiting Shawbost

We were always deemed late or if not late then too early,
as the door of Shawbost opened framing Morag,
chiding us not to trip on one of Agnes's cats hovering
on the threshold of perhaps the only house in Brookfield
that welcomed strays with more joy than the well heeled.
Bustled in with brusque absolution for our un-timeliness,
greeted in Gaelic by a voice from another room as
then wreathed in smoke Agnes would appear chittering
and soliciting news of health and irreverent living.

They would hover around the groaning table, oatcakes
and tea and a gaggle of disagreeing sisters all wrapped
in an island Mother's house. The artefacts of three
women's lives in scattered abandon, antiques and
bridge books piled high as they squeezed around, neither
sitting yet encouraging more intake as if we were gastronomic
gladiators; 'we who are about to burst salute you'.
Never could we make an exit without a thrust bundle of
supplies; perhaps a butchers' pie and of course a box of oatcakes.
Now as the last one passes we honour these two self-reliant
weavers home-spinning with Hebridean tweed and Paisley plaid.

The house named for a Lewis village is quieted now,

the cats drift away and the kettle is cold.

But these women who never wore the white veil

had a bond to family and hearth that birthed

an abundance of kindnesses, brushed over with modesty.

Who loved a brother in his industry and grind as if

the name of Malcolm was too high an honour to abandon.

Sisters in the struggle of life, wedded to the hospitality

that welcomed nieces and nephews, cats and all weathers.

May your welcome outlive your frailties by a hundred years

and when we seek that threshold between this life and the other

may we see you framed together in the doorway calling us home.

For Agnes & Morag Malcolm

Evacuee

I imagine you standing there on the platform
with your label and your gas mask strung over your shoulder,
excited to be travelling, chattering with friends.
Then tearful, startled at that first shunting movement
as the train judders, gasping steam, pulling you away from home,
away from the blitz and the bomb laden skies over London.

I still have your label, posted back from Northampton,
the first hard evidence reaching my Grandparent's doormat
of your safe arrival in unfamiliar lodging, such a gap of waiting.

Now when I locate a sudden departure in my life,
where the present state of things demands a moving on,
I pray to that little evacuee, the Mothering all latent in her
child's womb, yet to be born from war's labour and my delivery.

Now, again, you have been evacuated and I have received
no hand-written label, no assurance of your safe arrival.
What do I tell your Grandchildren still missing the woman
who sang them songs from the war, with calm assurances of peace?

Is it perhaps that the lengthening gap of absence, the empty chair
that must have filled your own Mother's Willesden terrace
and now sits in the corner of our unvisited Sunday afternoons
is your presence, rendering our deliveries and departures hopeful?

Does absence becomes presence, a sacrament of holding—
latent as I evoke you now and a young girls hand slips into mine?

Uncle

One of a dying breed.

He lay there, my Uncle,
the quiet man, waters running
deep like Clint Eastwood.

Hip replaced, stoical as ever,
grateful for our visit, I had never
seen him look so vulnerable before.

A man from Sheffield, Universal
Grinder in the Steel Works and then
when they shut them down; a Fireman.

Leading Hand, driving the appliance
into untold, always untold, dangers.
Allotment earth under his nails, sundark
skin and peaceable joy in growing things.

Once when I set fire to a garden conifer
and some other Firemen came; I said

you were my Uncle, and they told me
everyone has one prat for a nephew.

But you have never flinched to stand tall
when life called for your calm strength,
or to joke and tease and lift my mood all
those thirty years from Dad's death to Mum's.

Too often your qualities are overlooked
because they are not brassy or grasping,
rather a steely South Yorkshire testament
to the power of staying still in rich loam.

You have been Neil to me, once my aunt's
second husband, but writing now—by heart,
I will use the word that was once awkward,
Uncle, because it holds an acre of gratitude.

For Tess

When I saw you walk down the aisle
behind a young and coffined husband
shouldering the ache of abandoned intimacy,
in the very church where you married him,
I realised it was time to write about death
facing it directly, without blanching.

You had a sudden death boy and I had
a sudden death Dad to my child, Mother
to my adult, leaving us slack faced by
their swift carriage and no by your leavings.

In the days after you look scooped out
gradually turning translucent, because
you had seen through the veneer that
says death can't find the ones you love.

Both of us have met the cold gaze
of that empty under earth cavity, caught
the echoes of voices, never to be heard
again in this continuance we call living.

Can it really be over? The silence says yes
but the wrench that leaves terrific scars
screeches no, as we box up their left things,
cleaning out the cupboards of ended living.

So what is this death we call passing?
They say it is a mystery, no shit, try this for mystery—
the green plastic tube of ash on the car seat
as I leave the Co-operative funeral directors,
all that is left of the body that birthed me.
Your man never came home from a Christmas night out
just stayed there in the restaurant till they found him.
For me this is the real *mystery*– that most of us carry on.

We live on with death as our only certainty, elbowing its
way into every day, uninvited counsellor, shrouded ever presence.

Its afterness not my issue, a sleep to fall into, no
It's the relentless farewells and unexpected partings,
those cut off points that sweep great crusts of my
carefully constructed persona down the drain of loss.

Maybe that's the point, but where is the revelation?

There have been no blinding lights, little intimation
from beyond the grave – how about you Tess?
You make me think again of that scooping out,
the risk of opening ourselves to it, hoping
that the hollowing leads to a new vacuity.

An emptiness to be filled; a rich vintage,
seasoned by the loss of the parted, the wine of our
resolve to hold faith with death's intoxication?

Then one day, stepping out of the husk of grief
we can carry this new and luminous self
into a world where dying is just admission,
entrance to a new and beckoning pilgrimage.

3
Tuscany

September 2010

Married Again

The bright Tuscan hills
lay in checkered vineyards,
as the path spread before our feet,

walking into the twenty first year
of marriage, recalling to us the aisle of
first consent. When ahead and unlooked for

a figure, aproned, approaching,
beckoning and biblical, opening
his strong earthen face and hands

overwhelming any doubt
that we were called to the
spreading bride-white forest table.

He, Dario, the local butcher
exuding unbridled invitation,
like Jesus fresh from the resurrection

drew our company
from the path to a glade
in which he was to marry in a weeks time.

Offering soft bread with
thymed lamb, pouring the Tuscan
red clemency, our watery hopes made wine.

Our hearts extending
beyond the fences of what
normally would hem in our life.

And then he went before us
into his own Galilee – Panzano,
his shop a white tiled grandfathered gift.

In the corner an old
statue, with a man's bare chest,
a butchers apron and a great bull's head.

Dario steps up
onto his butchers block
atop the white counter's cliff,

Dante's Canto springs
from him like an oratorio
all sweeping arms and passion

And the story, Francesca and Paulo's
forbidden love, rich like strong meat
a weeping butcher in the second circle of hell.

After, we stood amazed,
dared by this man of earth
to enlarge the compass of our appreciation.

Married again to soil and beast,
soul and sorrow, dust and death, blood
and life, knowing ourselves to be consummated.

And this renewed marriage more
beguiling than the first, daring us
to believe in the wonder of our own walking.

Falling

The Italian week uncurled
like a tight packed fern frond,
each day a new disclosure
replicating an unlooked for
earthy Tuscan generosity.

Yet in some cynical corner
of your autobiographical memory
a presentiment of that stomach
churning lurch, that upending
rug pull endured, lurking.

Too many early losses
producing a canker of distrust,
a balance sheet approach that says
everything good will have to be
paid for in a painful coinage.

As you slid down the hill
on that final day, guard down,
it happened. The electric fence
protecting the ripe vineyard
was propped open with a stick.

You crouched and thrust a leg
through the aperture of freedom
only to kick the stick and slip
back, hand and full weight on
the horse kick of shocking current.

You knew it immediately for
the moment of retribution,
the payment to the ferryman,
body drumming with energy and
embarrassment, your luck run out.

Yet in the circle of reflection
on the morning of departure
you saw all the rug pulls in another
light and a voice said 'you know
there is great power in your falling'.

The providence of upheaval opened
Its generous hand to you, reworking
the territory of the past—exposing
that the presence in loss is the
impudent sprouting of a new life.

Mendicant

mendicant ˈmɛndɪk(ə)nt adjective
given to begging, of or denoting one
of the religious orders who originally
relied solely on alms.

I looked for a home

and the Earth raised

up lodgings to house

my unroofed soul.

I looked to find my way,

a course to chart and

the sea lent my self's ship

the meniscus of identity.

I looked for a helpmate

and the moon's curve

slid down to me a spouse

to cup my life's exposure.

I looked for a work

and the Sun gripped my

frame and warmed me

to a ploughing task.

I looked, fearfully, for
what I'd lost or exiled
and the forest gave me
its darkest, hardest truth.

I took the hand of defeat
as the harbinger of change
and in that frightful clinch
my emptiness was filled.

One day I will look for rest
and the chance to change
this span for another and
life will give me death.

Don't presume this way is easy;
to be mendicant; your hands
must be always emptying,
your skin always shedding,

you walk in second innocence,

you breath each day as new,

you renounce the chimera of control,

and make your heart a begging bowl.

4
Unearthings

The Pond

The pump malfunctioned
at exactly the wrong time,
late February when icing over
is still a constant danger.

I was shocked to step out
and find the whole surface
of the pond thick with a
frozen crust like an icy pie.
Trapped beneath this and
coldly baked were all the
frogs that arrive each year
to engage in mating, leaving
their tapioca of spawn lacing
the water with potential tadpoles
and subsequently a newness
of frogs—but not this year.

The worst part of the affair
was that when the water was
released from its hardness, in

turn it released all the dead frogs,

about one hundred of them,

and they began to rot and putrefy,

poisoning the pond, killing

all but one of my goldfish.

I had to don high wading wellingtons

and long rubber gloves made for

the purpose and step into the pond.

The smell was fetid, causing retching,

as I bucketed out frogs and water

right down to the mud at the bottom.

My one remaining fish swimming

in its little plastic bucket of tap water.

The bodies of the frogs had to be

burned on a bonfire, the plants reseated

and then finally a generous refilling;

returning the golden fish to its solitary water.

The pond slowly has come back to life

I bought a new pump, bigger and better,

and more companions for my fish

the little ecosystem rebalanced itself.

This year the frogs returned, fewer
in number but just as wanton and
producing as much spawn as before
the frog's apocalyptic icy cull.
I meet too many people who have
never cleared their ponds after a malfunction
and they stink of frog carcasses.

Accompaniment

accompaniment |əˈkʌmp(ə)nɪm(ə)nt noun
a musical part which supports or partners
an instrument, voice, or group

You come to me one by one,

to sit and talk, cup in hand,

straight backed or curled

like a bud, feet tucked up,

no frayed edges. Sometimes

you lay, almost prone, reaching

back into a submerged past,

or on the edge of your seat

straining towards a future

you suddenly glimpse.

What am I to you all?

An accompaniment,

as utterly present as I

can manage my self to be.

A fleshed and blooded mirror,

my own polished flaws

offering a mediated image
of the self you ache for,
your hidden desire,
even your exiled life.

This self that in the ebb
and flow of conversation;
offers you its truest smile
or your keenest grief, a chance
to live the life reflected back.

The question I have for you
who visit my waiting chair:
can you grasp the reckless
courage invited by this
simple act of vulnerability?

Can you persevere and
search out the children lost
down painful cul-de-sacs,
until they are found, and
their wounds are dressed?

Will you draw in that deep breath
of your inspired desire, the
one that most intoxicates you?
And then let the out-breath be
an assent to travel with what is
revealed in this lovely moment.

That moment of recognition
that its song was always
within you but because of the
accompaniment you are now
ready to stand up and sing it.

Annunciation (digitally)

The bee buzz of the text at three sixteen
ante meridiem (am), has my finger sweeping the
screen to disclose its message,

the glow of it lit my stooping face
like a renaissance nativity, my countenance
glowing in the bliss of annunciation.

This birth announced
was my cousin's daughter, a new pair of eyes
to reflect our world back to us,

the news so pristine
that its trill and glimmer reached me
right across the Irish Sea.

And so it is, that when those
pink fingers wiggle almost every family
becomes holy, for a while,

but as she grows it is the mirror
of our eyes that will show the child the truths or lies
we hold or coddle.

This reflective aspect
of our gaze is not a frozen surface, rather it is
the dark cusp of the currents of our life,

under it broods everything
we are and our children will see it all, be sure
they name it as they grow.

All we can do is sift
the flow of our days, all those silted bends, the more
mud dredged the purer the reflection,

and then what we can live together,
each day, will have the vigour to create the radiance
of empathy in which all children thrive.

For Amy Peggy Anson—Born 5th November 2011

Visits to Laugharne at Fifteen and Fifty

Fifteen

I came to Wales in a young pup body,
chiming like the first peels of a valley
chapel Sunday-best bell, to the lyric,
school learned lines of drunken Dylan,
an unfathered son twisting
down the ring rhyming valleys
to Carmarthen Bay, becalmed in
an Auntie's snug Ferryside terrace.
I asked to be sailed to Dylan's town
to remedy the stretched out, teenage,
bored boy, late rising days and
unsleeping, book reading nights.
Arriving to the thunderous drum
of the Pendine guns, ominous
like an impending front-line
advancing on my stripling youth.
In Laugharne was his writing shed,
as he left it, the chair hung coat,
screwed up lines wrinkling

dustily on a shabby rugged floor.
I hungered to gather those flung
away leaves, to unfurl, to touch
the dry bud of meaning, to harvest
his sowing, be my ego's own poet.
But the fleeting dab shine was
snatched away in a wing beat by the
heron's priestly stab, my meager
lines cast at fast receding tides.

Fifty

Now in my dog-eared years, signed
up late for pen to paper shoveling,
I return to the scruffy bard's Boathouse,
his unchanging empty bottled shed,
and his scroungy debt ridden paunch,
sponging from any he could tap,
yet singing in the cockle cobbled streets
the tom-tit tunes he milked from the wood.
I hunch at his parlour table drinking
municipal tea, the mock radio booming
out his reading voice, the sonourous Swansea
prophet soaring over the visitor's shortbread.

Fifteen and Fifty

They say a glimmer in the teens can

glisten at fifty, so here in his house I

turn the cog and whir of running verse,

winding again the spent spring of youth.

Then later on standing high at the end of

his birthday's walk staring back down

age's track, all seasoned by Dylan's

visceral candour, and his October blood.

So sharp and sheer I even see the shine in

his white cross grave, that has shone at me

since my lamb like days from an instamatic photo

I took as a boy when death meant nothing.

Caitlin is with him now, their drinking done,

words all spent, yet Dylan calls me again

in graveyard rain to sound each sputtering

slip or sprain, each kiss and whisper.

Not in the high flying, swallow-tailed

flights but in mole blind, hill making,

soft pawed earth does the splendor shine

blithering through from broken falls.

In a beaten down cheap mini market town,

I have seen hints in the lines on benches

and signs, how words wake the wounds

and wonderful seams concealed in mines

way below ground, in the heart's soil

that only the grave haunted brave with

lamp lit candle lines are able to burrow,

their seam gleaning grubbing the glinting flints.

Dylan's Grave

He was buried steadily before his death

by the weight of his drunken, unfaithful sins,

all that was left were his words and this white

wooden cross—solitary in a grandeur of granite.

But believe me his faith in the summer

of singing is richer by far than the cautious

yew ridden church that stoops over his grave,

with her half grasp of the beast bellied Christ.

A faith I have found in the pilgrim tracks of

each heart's foraging, to be sung at fifteen and

fifty, that our wounds are our glories and shall

be rung with his great poet's bell at dawn and dusk.

A Bigger Picture

I view Hockney's Bigger Picture,
tracks winding into infinity,
seasons of arboreal tunnels
their ending coming closer.

The irascible smoker's
vision of immortality;
'if this life is a mystery
why not the next one,
even greater', he quips.

I too declare my faith in beauty
with a Yorkshire accent,
and can spend whole mornings
gazing down a puddled lane.

His interviewer asked
tell me what you see,
'I can't, I'll paint it' he brushes,
canvass wolds, sun-drenched,
roads—light stippled and blossoming.

I suddenly trace the bigger picture
with my pen following his brush,
it reads in bold colour 'be *here*,
not in some fearful exit you can't predict.'

Here is the revelation of what life
feels like in a luminous lane,
or the bare copse of a Woldgate winter,
here celebrates the path's infinity
even though we take our leave of it.

This then is the bigger picture; we are part,
not of a blinkered dismal smallness,
but the Hockney bold, both barrels blazing,
life affirming glory of enormous trees.

Written after seeing David Hockney's Exhibition
and accompanying DVD both called the Bigger Picture
The Royal Academy
2012.

Christ Before the High Priest

Gerard van Honthorst (1590-1656)—The National Gallery

The canvass glistens on the gallery wall
where Honthorst has captured the light
of one solitary, recently lit candle.
Two figures are cast into relief by the
yellowing glow; Caiaphas and Christ.
The High Priest's index finger is raised
in pointed accusation at the kindnesses
that love in all its prodigality permits.
The book of judgment open before him
a ledger to the tyranny of perfection.
The accused Messiah suffers with a
patience that softens all harshness,
the candle's glare diffused by his distance
from it and his comfort with shadows.
Having just been hauled up out the
dungeon in which he witnessed all
of the High Priests' banished darkness.
Yet he still returns his fearful stare
with an unbounded compassion.

From where you stand on the polished floor

can you see the whole of the painting?

Can you encompass your own verdicts

alongside a daring embrace of

your own hidden, dungeoned darkness?

Can you step boldly into the scene;

the wrinkled agedness of your tired

Caiaphas — too close to the fierce flame

burning himself and all around him?

Can you catch the lowered gaze of

divine possibility that looking kindly

into the fierce eyes of your own

judgment and emerging from its prison

might be your next unshrinking step?

That is what Honthorst's Christ is ready for

though he has recently sweated blood.

Death Lodge

'Although the new story stirs inside them,
they know the old one must be laid to rest'
Bill Plotkin—Soulcraft

Black and White Stone

Standing before the cairn

asked by the guide

to choose a stone from

the remains of the past,

a singular pebble;

both black and white

from an ancient melting

arrived in my palm.

It's reminder of my

drive to divide into

welcomed or shunned,

carried in my pack up

towards Beinn Dearg.

The climb; tussock

hampered, every path

a watercourse, onto

the secluded upland.

Tent pitched between
two streams, standing
over forty hours of sitting
by the flow of water.
My first work to audit
the story to be laid to rest,
to allow the skin to shed,
ponder the stone's
darks and lights and
grasp my split parts.
Then to plunge under
the freezing cold of
the stream's joining,
placing the stone into
a fluid grave. Entrusting
the divided self to the
ever washing, wearing
away of acceptance.

Altar Stone

Then slow stepping
up under the crag of
Beinn Dearg, heather

purple peak with
high flying falls.
Crossing the plateau
to gape into the next
fold of land, rows of
corried cauldron hollows.
A landscape magical
when viewed for no other
reason than presence.
Drifting back to
my tent, dwarfed
by the high lands,
I step up to a broad
boulder—altar stone
to nature's vastness.
A place necessitating
vows instinct told me,
she also told me to wait.
Today relish the sunlight
and look ahead into
the future this landscape
imagines inside you.
Then sleep in the arms

of two streams and

become a confluence

of regret and hope.

Waking again to the

quietly tapping fingers

of June snow peppering

the translucent skin

of my nylon lodging.

Pushing through the neck

of the tent's womb from

the swaddle of dreams

into dawn's cloudy breath.

Amazed by the crag's

snowy head, more amazed

by the tender eye of a soft

doe catching mine as she

stands alone by the altar stone.

Green Eyed Stone

My final task to yield

to the summons in her

gaze and name myself

as vowed to a future.

Nearing the altar stone
she melts away, a small
moss eyed stone sits neatly
atop the rock and then
in my hand. No longer
am I split, but singularly
ocular, holding one vision
arising inside me as the
annunciation of a vow.
'By all this rough cut
beauty I vow to shape
myself to a poetic
urgency, the primary
demand to voice
all that strikes a note
in me—sharp or flat.
To gather counsel for
myself and others—
pilgrims to uncertainty.
To name when the seer
turns tyrant and find
raw guides for the way.
To be a more gracious

recipient of the love

I already possess and

never close the door

on its unmet face.'

Miraculous to me a lark

rises behind and above

voicing my vow's melody.

As prone over the boulder,

I sob out a lachrymose

seal on my fiercely

vulnerable vows.

Rinsed, I return down

the mountain, with the

green eyed stone—the seed

of the newly sown

story stirring inside me.

The Girdled Tree of Eyam

Walking out from Eyam you pass a girdled oak,
its iron cage once armour against the grazing cattle,
as the sapling grew, what once protected has
cut deep into the tree as bark heals over iron.

This village where the plague was checked in
its greedy tracks by the will and testament of
those who, with roses in a ring, fell down to
free life's tree from its noisome cage by dying.

Not that they rid the whole trunk of its painful pen,
instead they allowed life to grow over death,
encasing it in a crust of offering, a covering of
suffering becoming a smooth and future bark.

I walk today with a found brother past the church
surrounded by its martyrs, staring in the windows
of the cottages of the damned who died so others
would be blessed, and out, out to the girdled tree.

We wonder what will we embrace as this tree
has embraced its coop, what will we allow to
constantly injure us, and how will we grow
the bark of acceptance, the rind of readiness?

These questions haunt us as Eyam's mystery
girdles us, incarnate in the magical visitation
of two tall horses, grey and brown, approaching
us intently with a delicate nuzzling power .

As we leave this place we know that we have
walked in magic, Emmaus reached, hearts
burning with a brotherhood that demands we stop
the plague of unreached manhood in its tracks.

A labour that is the burden of this wounded place
to oppose the contagion of unconscious living,
where men are constantly wounded and wounding,
to be a summons to the way of beckoning awakening.

In many years, when we are gone others will
pass this tree and never realise that ironwork
became a corrupted sanctuary only to find
itself overwhelmed by adamant wildness.

5
Glad Arrivals

Blossom

As you drive past
the hanging blossom of the cherry tree,
you are moving too fast.

Their pale luminescence an unnoticed glory,
a promise, year by year, you fail to keep.

But one day soon you will stop,
get out of the car
and amble down the aisle of spring.

There you will feel
the tidal pull of all that growth,
the vernal current of possibility.

It will be time to call an end to speed
and the unspoken grimness of hurry.

What will the blossom say
as it falls kindly on your upturned face?

'You are my witness,

your presence a sign that falling is never wasted.'

Look the strewn confetti of a richer life

is all around you, all you have to do

is trust its kindness to bring you home.

Then you will see; there is no other life for you,

hidden in someone else's wake.

Only this marriage to everything you meet

on the roughened track covered in blossom.

Only to welcome yourself as a guest

at these unexpected nuptials of self compassion.

Only this spring, your own spring,

blossoming open before your astonished face.

Silence

Silence is a Spring within me
a blossoming visitation,
coming as it does from such
a generous, hidden origination.
It houses my long gazing child
and reads my grown-up fears,
always discerning my readiness
for the revelation that appears.

Silence has made a home in me
since my early dreaming reveries,
but panic filled my rooms like
the hoarder stuffing memories.
Yet the stillness invites me
to relish their edgy company,
embrace their awkward solidarity
as they acquaint me with my life.

Silence makes no judgments,
yearns for full attention,
expects a long held courtship

breathes through distraction.
It is not the absence of sound
but the quieting of my chatter,
deft moment of receptivity
sudden doorway to sensuality.

Silence I came from,
into silence I will go, now
the seed of quiet is quivering,
ready to fall into my waiting.
Dreams that give life grow
from this tender germination
and life worth living comes
from catching its invitation.

The Circle

This space formed by gathering,
is unmindful of social grading,
repelling all attempts at control
and when held with intention
is the embrace of invention.

It echoes in archeological rings,
ancient signs from before the kings
when once we trusted its magic
within Stanton Drew and Callanish,
Stonehenge, the solstice sun's rising kiss.

An easily convened circularity
that the managers of linearity
deform into a triangle
with a self appointed pinnacle
that they sit at, shrewd and cynical.

But this is the great O of wonder,
not to be exploited for plunder,
entered with listening and speaking

never both, never simultaneously,
as the soul arises spontaneously.

Sit in the circumference of infinity
submit to a way that yields acuity,
a vision that each can lay claim to,
their presence in the circle a harvest
the bounty of being truth's hearth guest.

I would defend this space with my life
when those who scorn its sway are rife
So how to hold its magic against those
whose brands are their banners unfurled
claiming it is not part of their real world?

Perhaps we don't have to defend,
perhaps we just have to let it befriend
the echoing spiral of our life's course
and then when the circle is done
those remaining in the circle are one.

There is a Stage

There is a stage
called the present moment
that you are constantly stepping onto.

If you concentrate you can sense
its curtain call just under your navel,
that union of courage and instinct.

A breathing anchor
that keeps you right here
in the present action of your life.

A whole cast crosses this space,
playing parts not listed in the jaded
program notes of your past.

Only by being centered
are you able to grasp their
roles in the current production.

Only by choosing to value your life
as a performance worth watching
will you start to catch its gist.

Only by acting your part with
utter conviction will you know that
you are not the only author of your lines

This peculiar kind of remembering,
is a calling forth, a reaching that releases
the brilliant self hidden in your wings.

For Eva

This is All the Life You Have

This is all the life you have,
each day's crests and furrows
promising that who you are
embodies all you will ever need.

So what, so often, convinces
you that you are inadequate,
is it others or more likely
your unbefriended failures?

Sit quietly in the morning
before one screen or another
can invade your day with
the software of deficiency.

Let the silence teach you that
solitude is not an illness,
it is the soil of breath taking
in which self-acceptance grows.

Believe in the bird's song,

and the way the sun rises, slowly,

the steady beat of your pulse,

at that pace you can love it all.

At that pace, unforced providence

offers each part of your life

to you and you can name it as

Eve and Adam named it all.

What you can name as loved

will bring freedom to your day

will uncover your fullness and

will finally take your breath away.

The Starving Edge

You ask me to write of new beginnings
    when from
    un-leaving trees
    autumn blood flows,
when the talk is all of cuts carving
    the trunk of consented life.

Such wanton speeches made sly solemnly
    by those
    sitting smug in
    the safest seats,
feed the juggernaut of greed, taxing
    fierce sacrifices from the frail.

Can vulnerable buds be induced at
    this blood
    wounded juncture?
    As heedless boots
cause a crunching carpet's golden leaves
    to break down to crumbling brown.

The bleeding of trees and the grieving of

    clouds names

    November's rise,

    month of recalled

souls, as a gusted gull croaks above

    the nets my words are casting.

Time to grieve the wounds that fester unsung,

    to find

    the silent rooms,

    the dormant tombs

that long lain unused could prove wombs to

    the remaking we ache for.

The true new beginning is to live stripped,

    willing

    and wilful at

    the starving edge

of brightening days, where solstice endured

    yields to winter birthing spring.

6
Walking On

There is a Certain Kind Of Vow

There is a certain kind of vow you can only make after
writing an autobiography.
Not to sell your image like celebrities do, but
chiseled with grinding honesty.
You do not have to publish—just be readable,
tell your story.
You do not even have to write it, just speak it aloud,
voice yourself in a plain simple admission.
Then, when you have it down, courageously recount it
to someone else.
Not just anybody, but one who has earned the rights
to your defenselessness.
When you have risked this step, then comes the avowal,
the profession.
St Francis, we are told made a profession of poverty
before the Bishop and his Father.
He renounced his clothes, going barefoot into that fierce
world of danger and nature outside the city.
Yours too, will be a self-sealed willingness to hazard yourself,
adventure into the grindstone of reality.
Francis called it poverty and then it was institutionalized, neutered,

I think we would call it vulnerability.

To take only that, which you have found in your story,

and walk out beyond your city wall.

There is a certain kind of vow that no one can make for you,

it is the vow of vulnerability.